Winter Oysters

Winter Oysters

POEMS BY
BRENDAN GALVIN

Athens
The University of Georgia Press

Copyright © 1983 by Brendan Galvin
Published by the University of Georgia Press
Athens, Georgia 30602

All rights reserved
Set in 10 on 12 point Monticello type
Printed in the United States of America

The paper in this book meets the guidelines for permanence
and durability of the Committee on Production Guidelines for
Book Longevity of the Council on Library Resources.

Library of Congress Cataloging in Publication Data

Galvin, Brendan.
    Winter oysters.
    I. Title.
PS3557.A44W5 1983   811'.54   82–13367
ISBN 0–8203–0643–6
ISBN 0–8203–0644–4 (pbk.)

The publication of this book is supported by a grant from the
National Endowment for the Arts, a federal agency.

Acknowledgments

Acknowledgment is given to the following publications in which poems from this book first appeared.

Ascent: "Just in Case You're Wondering Who You Are," "A Few Words from the Weeds," "August"

The Georgia Review: "Saying Her Name," "Old Woman Telling Another Version"

Harvard Magazine: "Approaching the Compost"

The New England Review: "Lying to Fall Warblers," "The Last Open-Air Concert"

New Jersey Poetry Journal: "Four at the Feeder," published originally as "Matins" in "The Secular Hours," "Barnum Locking Up," "General Confession of the Ex-King of Hamburg"

The New Republic: "Nose," "A Double-Ended Dory"

The New Yorker: "Listening by a Woodpile, Night of Moon after Snow," "Transmigration"

Poet Lore: "Reading the Obituaries," "Hitting the Wall"

Poetry Northwest: "Marsh," "Explaining a Fiend to My Daughter," "The Renting Coloratura"

Prairie Schooner: "An Old One" (© 1982 University of Nebraska Press)

Quarterly West: "Becoming a Dump Keeper"

The Sewanee Review: "Lost Countrymen," "July," "The Brueghel Moment," "Owl-Struck"

The Southern Review: "Mole," "Pack Ice"

Tar River Poetry: "After Fifteen Years," "The Grackles"

Three Rivers Poetry Journal: "Winter Oysters," "Dog Love," "Mrs. McCandless," "Today You Will Meet the Love of Your Life," "The Mockingbird," "Listening to Maine Public Radio," "With Anne at the Peabody"

Thanks to the Connecticut Commission on the Arts for a grant which aided in the completion of this book, and to the Research Council of Central Connecticut State University, especially Dean W. R. Brown, for time off during which some of these poems were written.

Contents

IV

For George Garrett and Tom Reiter

I

Saying Her Name

Women who heard
Pipsissewa
on the lips of dreaming braves
had sufficient tribal grounds
for divorce.

She was so beautiful
no man was allowed to sleep
and remember her,
and when she died for love
this is the flower
that appeared over her grave.

I have been spinning
elaborations
about this low-growing evergreen
for days:
how they gave it
the consolation of her name,

how the flower
seems to hover above meadows,
how the sepals, brewed by lovers
and drunk from a single cup,
insure fidelity.

I have made all this up
out of a crooked need
to deepen truth:
the last Pamet Indian

lies with his myths
somewhere around here,

and taller than hog cranberry,
in this pine shade beneath
the notice of herbalists,
Pipsissewa grows.

Its flower looks at the ground,
so, in my version,
it remembers. And when
I slip a finger under its chin

and look it in the eye,
someone muffled in me
as in a quilt
steps out saying her name.

Old Woman Telling Another Version

She begins as if memory were faultless,
some lost June where you just step off the pavement
to a cart track through locust groves,

smiling in that watery green-gold light
until you look back
where leaves have come together,
screening what would have been
your way out.

        Now you're in it
to the end, and the way's deepening,
shadowy with overhung pines,

though the double track's still hard clay
where rains have run the sand off,
and the walking's easy till you see
that up ahead the names will be borrowed
from the graveyard of faceless ones.

You've been here, or somewhere similar,
before: it's familiar as
the redolent drift from a bush
deep in the field beyond those trees,

something someone planted
when that single clapboard wall
and three others made home.

How long before you know it: that only
a composer could map this tale,

that no cartographer could join its broken
lines and cross-country leaps?

These wild wisps of asparagus growing
through a rusted screen,
rudiments of the garden that was here;

flashes like the orange of day lilies
strayed into a bog; certain facts
skirted like kettle holes that cup
sunless water; the point that
there is no point . . .

                    Out of love or sorrow
or simply to honor the teller,

though any move may involve you to your knees
in guilt and shame, in potholes
mouldering leaves to a slush
like grade-school ink,

you go on to arrive sweat-soaked
in another month or year,
your clothes outgrown or torn at by wild canes,

burrs and scarecrow chaff at wrist and ankle,
empty among the black
flap-ups of denunciation,

while she sits where quail
call to each other across the pond,
and nothing can be done.

An Old One

How bad can it be
to have one mouth for
drinking the rain
and another for speaking it back
as birds,

to have hollows
a hermit could live in,
to be seen through,
yet remain
the destination of bees
who dust off
and whisper their news?

Come fall, this apple tree
strips to branches like
hysteria's hair,
waits for a saint of the folk
to trim it back,

and hangs out the sour,
cramped lights
of its disposition
till they drop and fester
into potable air.

Springs when you feel
you won't feel springs again,
petals touch
the silk under your ribs.

Listening to Maine Public Radio

On blue days
each note drops out of the air
to this wrist of Massachusetts
without hesitation,
the same concerto
heard in places I've never seen,
Presque Isle, Shin Pond, Lubec,
names I love the way
I love haying reports
from a station in a cloud,
from a state overhanging
this corner of the country
like a cumulus
building into the Maritimes.
But today, static in sleets
and intermittent surfs,
as though thundershowers
had shambled down
out of the White Mountains
to walk Stellwagen Bank,
as though Bartok's thoughts
were bouncing in skysails
over the sea's place-names.

A Double-Ended Dory

You may never understand
why I shoveled the zinnias out of her
after closing time, looking over
my shoulder for cops, if you've
never put offshore
in anything but a hull like tupperware.
But she sat out the calm
in front of the Chowder House,
a hangdog flower bed
sad as a thoroughbred pointer
wearing a Christmas bow.
Her gunnels were hand-shaved,
her strakes had been soaked to fitting
curves, and when I dug out
her ribs and knees, they still evoked
arches and buttresses. Once she was
tight as a pod, clinker-built
for cod-lining on the Banks:
the deeper the fish in her bins,
the surer she sat two men
in the troughs between waves.
Remembering coves where her corners
might still hold rain
and a plankton swirl, I got one end
up on the tailgate, then shoved
feeling hope throw its weight in
with mine, and took the old county road.

The Renting Coloratura

In the stillness
after a marsh fox cried,

she struck the first note:
a tinny string pegged to some ancient frame.

They were no words we knew,
but a lament
steeped in Mediterranean longing.

Revenge flashed a blade
among olive trees, marine evening
trembled with broken love.

That was the first night.

Since then we have decided
there's no song, only unending plangency
without a plot or tryst, without beginning,

middle, sword, or denouement,
landscapeless, played out in the theater
in the round beneath the hair,

the vehicle, somebody's rickety piano,
its strings slack as a hammock
snow has slept in.

And she who launches such exploding larks,
flummoxing night, must pay

the summer rental on a glossy octagon

among these hills, well-lit,
whose double panes and sliding doors,

thrown back, return her favored
versions of herself.

What grief is this, playing to the packed hall
of our frustrations, until one Bravo,
blocking his own flops,
applauds her nightly from a redwood deck?

First of the month is here, and she stays on.
Things will go on like this
until the night one of us calls the cops.

Hitting the Wall

Woodpecker, black-and-white
downy, ladder-backed red-capped
male, now that the rolling
terror is over, wait,

as I waited this morning
after pushing myself through
too many miles in a valley
that trapped sun on the river road.

Soaked as though I had run
under the river,
I pushed myself uphill
to the point where a beached fish
panicked in my chest.

I have collared and dragged
the cat away, subtracting it
from your pulse rate. Let time
rest like a compress
on your forehead. We've been
to the edge today,
and seen the ground waiting.

Now there's the wisdom
of merely holding back, until fear
lies down in your breath
and your beak doesn't have to work
for air anymore.

I am with you, walking
each step of your runaway

heartbeat down, reliving
the morning. Don't fly!

Make time for the future's
drift from limb to limb. The way
this morning I eased myself
branch by branch
up the embankment. Here.

July

"Self-realization,"
"the pursuit of happiness,"
seem illuminated when wings
wrinkle out of thumb-sized turbans
and butterflies hang,
drying before they attempt
a month of air. Who will say
this intensity isn't a surfeit,
that the spider, rigging its bellyful
where bees plunge to their shoulders
in lusciousness, doesn't view
creation as democratic?
But after the final eight-legged
embrace, when the rage
of downward thralldoms appears
in remission, we are apt to remember
stories: how someone's father's
father, deep in public works, struck
through planking to a glass
coffin lid, how his fist unlocked
at the perfect little girl, how
his shovel dropped and the air
billowed dust through a stiff white dress.

Approaching the Compost

Getting there is like stepping into
one of those hidden pictures
wherein children discover
that trees contain a giraffe,
that a bird, turned
upside down, has another bird
in its wing. Therefore
I approach warily, coming past
pine stumps who overreached themselves
until aspiration snapped
and they hunkered down,
letting what happens
happen. Now they are wood trolls,
menschen, tenants of
orphaned water who've earned
their faces. *To pass, guess my name,*
each seems to say, and I get by
Quail Pulpit, who next week
or tomorrow may be changed
into Owl Hat. Always prepared for
the wrong event in the wrong place,
I raise the gates of caution
when I come face-to-face
with a good gray bristle of filaments.
Now I'm getting reeks
that could bring anything to earth,
whiffs of dismantled snow, a matrix of
fishtails in league with barn muckout
and falls that blew down
in an hour. Already the acolyte crows
have heard about my bucket of addenda,
and are ripping their cries
from the background arras of song.

The Mockingbird

Far into moonlight he tries
to recall his own song,
but a whippoorwill
floats out three notes
wobbly and clear as bubbles,
so he corrects them for her,
melding them with a child's
creaky swing, but erases
that line, and takes a new tack
from a siren on route 17,
then drops to a cowbird
like water poured into water.

This business of getting
the world right
isn't for dilettantes; when
the voices fill you,
you must say nothing wrong,
but follow them back
through the day, going phrase
by phrase over hills,

pausing here and there on a pole
to help goldfinches chip
the sun to a perfect wheel,
dropping by underleaf stones
to improve on mandalas
a cricket's printing in air,
and waiting at cedar posts
to teach killdeer
to pronounce their own names better.

You must bring it all back
alive as the repertoire
of your inner ear,
past fences and over stones,
through one face of leaves
and another
to someone awake on the outskirts,

this woman propped on a pillow,
beginning to see, among fifes,
in her darkened room, a band
dressed like Blue Caballeros.

You must help her imagine
sun living on brass horns,
and an easy, foot-saving march
as the ensemble passes,
air in its wake
banged to a bass difference.

After Fifteen Years

Before we have sullied our tongues
with Stearoyl-2-lactylate,
and our eyes and ears with the news,
and our arches with Dr. Scholl's,
before we're straight-armed
by multinationals, and disapproval
lets out its dogs for the day,

we go out in our Adam and Eve
Galvin suits, common as potato
blossoms, past raspberries
like wee contemplatives' cells,
and I try not six, or four,
but five blueberries from your hand
for the rush of sky-colored
angels through my chest.

Marsh

Small, nameless hole
I first located by amphibian groans
and the gut-plucking
you send through face-high reeds,
you are your own system and mystery.

I come here to admire
an economy I don't understand:
how you focus everything,
gathering runoff,

feeding out highbush blueberry,
foxgrape, fescue, mallow,
and poison ivy, reclaiming the wheelruts
worked in around you.

Yesterday's waterlogged rat
is gone, but that pizza box has been
dragged further in, perhaps
by the ebony hand that piles
ripe strawberries under
leaves. If I threw you a can
or plastic, you'd go to work on it.

Daily, above seeds
of swimming light (killies,
mummies, bluegill, fry),
you send a small green heron
out to sea,

and from your matrix under mud,
up through teeming,

microscopic herds
that look like cave drawings of bison,
you exist to be eaten.

You exist to be eaten
to the tallest cattail tip,
and your eaters eaten.

Still, you are here again today,
undiminished, preventing me
from that far bank of *rosa palustris*
backed with gold dune
and blue distance,

offering
a womb's worth of pink-footed mice
gray as old peanuts.

Four at the Feeder

An oak leaf pawing air
or a single snigger escaping the dark
and I surface, listening for the cat's
baby cry to be let in, hoping
there'll be no half dollar of fur
torn from her haunch, no burnt-tire
whiff of skunk making my breath
back off as far as my molars.

But those nervous chuckles and hoots
mean only one thing: raccoons.
Four at the feeder, climbing
each other to paw out sunflower seeds.
This spring's brood, their new fur
nappy, still not sure
in their minor bear-shapes.

Two leave quickly. Winters, I've caught
their mother or grandfather like this,
fangs in the suet. The third, following,
spits over his shoulder and stares,
the adolescent hothead who'd slice
this screen like cheesecloth.

Partway up a pine, the last one's
bandito face taunts from one side then
the other. He wobbles off
to become one with the grass.

An overlay of mist on the marsh,
soft as sherbet, and birds sipping
the momentary limelight. At my footfall
two mourning doves titter away,
girls caught initialing
a heart on a sidewalk.

The Grackles

From a dream of armor collapsing,
the clatter of helmets and greaves,
gauntlets crashing on stone,

I woke knowing they were back,
their cries gleaned from homestead gates
the wind on the northern rim
of America toys with.

If it were only one or a few
such as all summer scuffled
in the huckleberry,

their failed storekeeper's eyes—
worry trapped in a bile-yellow
ring of anger—taking the inventory
of underleaf lives,

but this morning so many moved so fast
from pokeweed to cutworm to acorns
they eluded count, outriders
flaked off a south-going cloud,

their feathers amalgamating steel-blue
and bronze, as though every bird
had been dipped in a lubricant
intended to soothe its cries into song.

All day they split

the gross contents of pods, twangling
like so many cash drawers springing open,

hoarding all they could carry
for their long haul toward the evening's
vast collision, where they would provide
the final clatter of chrome.

August

In the town where I grew up
they wedge me at a table
next to our hostess, Lila Dalhouser,
ex–Martha Graham dancer,

this evening nursing a black eye
she caught from unknown matrons
in a knock-down drag-out
for a parking space at Old Cove Beach,

and to my right, Susannah Lesch,
The Edna Millay of New Billingsgate,
who's looking for a chance to say,
"Perhaps life *is* only a series
of late-night collisions."

Our hostess's blouse seems loosely
stitched of old lace curtain,
and somehow has commenced unbuttoning.
The evening wears, her peekaboo
and shiner combination
reminding me of Provincetown bar waifs.

But now a bug is wandering among
dishes of cuisine Cantonese (à la Dalhouser),
A Manhattan Cockroach! cries Dr. D.,

here in the town where I grew up,
where every wall without a window
is an art gallery, and Eduardo Caballo,
action painter, entertained two hookers
in a beach towel on his fiftieth,

gifts of his missus, who tells it
as a civic improvement.

What this party needs is
Ricky Dill, of Bottled Gas Delivery
by day, by night a Country-Western
singer, hell on teenage girls,

and Edgar Sledd, of Village Taxi,
humpbacked, but once the shortstop
on a Red Sox farm club.

But here's Arshile "Pucky" Deveaux,
Iowa City Ballet, now of La Galleria,
known for his charcoal studies of
New Billingsgate boys,

and Jack Skow, handsome builder of
Big Sur Look Living Spaces,
Whitmanian in beard and cowboy hat,
telling the Dalhousers why their new house
is like a boat, how rain tightens the seams,

how, once they understand
the Functionality Concept, they'll never
never use the word "ugly" again.

This party needs at least a busload
of the batty poets, dressed in
20s football gear—Schwartz, Roethke,
Vachel Lindsay, and Charles Olson,

big guys in floppy shoulderpads

and earflaps, batting the screens outside
like moths for light.

I'd let them in to hear
McDonald Ledyard, Mathematical
Revisionist, explaining why,
in theory, diagonals don't work.

Tonight I'll come to, late,
some summer native or two-week rentee's
doberman or malamute circling
my foundation, staking claims,

but happy if I hear
one cricket oiling up,
beginning to saw the base posts
of this summer.

II

Transmigration

When your bones turn
loose and light as a deck chair
and you raise a rickety
blue pavilion over yourself,

beginning to see from above
how a breeze
ignites marsh grass every-which-way
to new greens,

at first fear will set you down
in the tip of an oak,
your new feet gripping.
Wait. Let instinct assure you
you look like only another
piece of sky between ragged trees.

So this is it.
Who would believe,
this late, this century. . . .

You were running the low tide—
a man in midlife
trying to shake off a pelt
built of too many
trips to too many troughs,
rightly accusing yourself
of having sat out easy rains.

Printing the glacial till
back of Egg Island,
threading pincer movements

of tide, making gulls thrash
water to light, you were
changed in a battering
wink of their wingstorm.

Put everything away.
As if this tree could suddenly
haul in branches and leaves,
you can take in your new wings,
becoming all trunk,
a long-necked sapling
up to the sun.

Then one white stump-crouch
and spring, arms wagging
a quick blue semaphore,
going away until, flat out on air,
that looseness again,
the lattice of bones sliding
above sinews of creeks.

What are you, a soul?
It seems easy to push
earth off and be a diver
exempt from gravity, to flap out
above hay wastes and revolve till
the airport runway could be
a dropped paperclip,

or to glide, a shadow across
hogbacks, for the first time
seeing the art of tractors,
and ocean at practice whittling sandspits,
piling silt like reflected cumulus.

And those ponds back of town,
stations of glacial water

worked by an underworld of
shifting twilights,
permanently cold because
they were shed from the icecap's
orphaned bergs: Little Duck,

a mirage through pines,
where you found the wild wintergreen
and kept a leaf on your tongue,
wishing for deer all the way
to its white shore,

and Ryder, whose beach
you curled up on with one summer's girl
long ago, and woke to Billy Morna,
Old Man Newcomb, the whole road crew
staring over the bank
like kids around a barrel of strange fish—

though such memories are useless,
you find you can go there
and stand in the pale bole
of this new shape, indulging
your hunger for swimming food.

And when blue hollows
invite deeper blues, and marsh
takes on the aura of
undersea fields, last light
drops off the planet's
easy curve, though you rise
in juddering bones to keep it.

What's this? A voice up here?
Voices. Crackles of speech
as off a police radio,
some river of air alive with rage

tearing itself to froth.
Industrial sump, guggle of
money talk shot through
the redolence of a barbecue.

As you pass through the vowels
of love, scenting flowers
whose names, now, you will
never get straight, you know
you will come here often
for snatches of the inconsequential
that bind person to person
and day to day below,

where Main Street seems to be lifting
moonward, and headlights run
out a few capillary roads
among dunes grained
like the surface of old bones.
Veering, you scout for
a sour updraft of pond.

And in the end, come to yourself
above roofs struggling unequally
out of leaves. Hearing bells
crosscut by rifts of wind,
and an organ thin as a harmonica.

Lifted from that pattern
you can't feel for what you trail
above familiar cars up Main Street,
Commercial, School Street,
arriving over Memorial Lawn,

and nothing you could say
to that veiled woman

and downcast kids would explain
this simple rightness of things.

The wind shifts, and as if
in a time lapse, maples begin
flaunting their reds. Arranging
the town off one wing, and sea,
squalling up, off the other,

you hang out on air until
white, blue white, yellow,
the cloud-pelted moon
drags up new stars, magnitudes
winking out of the portside dark.

III

With Anne at the Peabody

In this house of the chemical error
and wronged bone, of things
that might waggle up
to the mudbanks of imagination's
wrong turns, triceratops' skulls
wait like the helmets of dream samurai,
and the eon-by-eon endeavors
of this world—particles incubated
to a crawl toward a dead end—
totter reason.

You've been here before, and rush me.
I can't absorb even the name
of a single age, though every one
could be called the Pleonastic:
I think of the ritual filing of
each tooth, the endless stringing
of bead upon bead, the minute-by-minute
urge of creation's tree,

and the tranced or slipshod
intensity of collectors,
stone dusters, those who risked
the local curse so this morning
600 kids can swarm to print glass
that protects a Samoan about to sling
a rock, his arm finely turned that way
after endless failures.

Take your time. As the dust of this world
sifts down and builds on our shoulders
as though someone were breaking through above,

your prized Egyptian girl, with her cup
of grain, will become someone's daughter
bought like a curio in Alexandria,

and those dinosaur bones
will seem to lean in pursuit
as though just ahead
they could slip back into the flesh.

Explaining a Fiend to My Daughter

A fiend is even worse
than the Frostbiter.

Think of yourself
as he thinks of you:

a funny rubber suit.
Up the wall he comes,

hands and feet as on
Grandma's furniture,

hair like a chimney fire
on a face that just

fell off a cathedral roof.
Once he gets under your skin,

he goes for your elbows
and knees. Days when you're

not yourself you get an inkling.
But a fiend does what he does,

so you always know where
you stand, or dance or fly.

"Actually, I'm surprised
to find myself here"

is something he'll never say,
and he doesn't close the door

and rifle your file, or
wear a suit that matches

the corridor wall.
No buts or surcharges,

no pungent asides to
the mailbox. He deals

his double whammies
without hiding in hedges

of euphemism, or creeping
around behind Abstraction's

outhouse.

Nose

Troublesome doorway, who can say
what wanderings you've given
hospice to, until one day
a conjunction of frying eggs
and east wind through locust trees
triggers a glitter—
Isaac Lane the eggman,
the wooden sides of his Model A wagon
looking edible as sugar wafers,
its motor a child puttering air
through closed lips, Isaac himself
a pastiche of suspenders
and mustache—and I reach
to touch a fender,
beyond it only air.

Lost Countrymen

When I stood in the glass drugstore
with the clerk who couldn't find anything
but the cash register,
the two of us caught in the air
inside a goblet ringing to shatter,
I remembered those men
who seemed to have climbed
out of the skysails
and short bunks of Whalers
after New Bedford shut down.
They came from houses behind
the little ponds, and walked
their grandfathers' trails
to gas pumps like old-movie robots,
and stores that sold everything.
While the boss wore a tie
and died fat, Norwell Fisher
climbed for fly swatters
and rum-soaked cigars, and knew
which tool would do what.
Asberry Paine's beagles,
who seemed to travel the town
under haloes, visited where he dug
a foundation hole in a single day.
They were men in shirt-sleeves
and bib overalls and high-topped
sneakers. They got on with it,
they did till the last day, and were
up to the irony of posing with tourists
who thought them rickety, back-country
Charlie Chaplins.
But those wiry getters and sweepers
are all gone now, and that clerk
is only a clerk, and can't help it.

Becoming a Dump Keeper

Keeping in mind the hazards
of shrinks and peeping toms,

begin by overlooking
everything: go delicate

and forgiving as the best
father confessor, your bent

for gossip as damp
as these acres. When others talk

they'll say you soften bottles
five cents at a time

for a mattress of legal tender.
Though paid like a librarian,

make up your mind to show
a face that shows you're dreaming

clouds of money; don't invent
a decimal system for

our dreck. No one will say
you're necessary as surgeons,

though you are. No one
will come one rainy afternoon

to help you trail the gull
muzzled with six-pack plastic.

If you blanket-trap it
you can snip the beak free,

but first you'll have to walk it
down to weakness—circling

love's pink slips, and a crow
wearing a lemon slice

like a smile—with the studied
patience learned from decay.

General Confession of the Ex-King of Hamburg

Fearing the cold chest's blue lights
were sterilizing more than Australian
lean beef, fearing even as I ground it
that it was frozen dingo, that I'd donate
a finger or someone would die
from chickens left in ice water overnight
to kill their smell, I who worked my way up
from junior produce clerk, the statute
of limitations having run out, time
having run out for four thousand employees
of the chain, confess to having heated
shrimp fried rice in the rotisserie on
slow nights. It was only because I was bored
with the art of looking busy, the hours
down cellar grooming sawdust into floor plans.
As to the twenty pounds I put on while in
your employ, I plead *nolo*, but I swear
I never ate cherrystone clams
with horseradish sauce those evenings.
Perhaps it was some meatcutter, tired
of the Super's stories of dummying
bullets at Chateau Thierry? It is true
that on lunch hours I cheered
through the one-way mirror for the shopper
who dropped Alka-Seltzer in her purse
and the student who lined his fatigue
jacket with chops, and was sad for the lady
kicking the floor, a manager and his
assistant holding her arms while she seemed
to deliver a Beltsville turkey. Now,
as electric eyes on fifty-two doors
blink into bankruptcy, and rats race

tarantulas for the hands of blackened bananas,
may marriage or early retirement have found
several meat wrappers I loved at respectable
distances from their rippled soles
to the tips of their paper tiaras.

Barnum Locking Up

The last squawks of the orchestra
have died unfledged on the pavement,
and the crowd is gone, who never expected
anything good for free anyway.

The take's counted and impounded,
the African Pinhead, suddenly
articulate with goodnights,
is let out to the wife and children.

In the Great American Museum, its floodlamps
and bubbling illuminations
off, the glass around the buccaneer
Tom Trouble's bloody arm
has been wiped of the Million's smears,

but alone among the Grand Cosmoramas
and the anaconda digesting
its bulge of rats,
Barnum remembers the noon
he followed his father's Irishman

north through the unmown portion
of meadow, toward trees awash with summer,
a boy's belief in the possible
chafing between his mother's homily
against pride of wealth

and his grandfather's speculation
that this boy
could be the richest in all Bethel.

Spongy ground obliged them
to step with care,
then leap tussock to tussock until
one sideslipped him
waist deep in bog,

unlodging a bee swarm
he couldn't dismiss from his face
the way he'd mopped
field itch and jewels of sweat.

But a quarter-mile across
that morass, beyond that screen
of alders: Ivy Island,
acreage his grandfather
Phineas Taylor had willed
this namesake at christening.

At the final stream
Edmund felled an oak, and they crossed over,
mudded, hung with duckweed,
and he stood for the only time
on his legacy of scrub and poison ivy.

He was ten, but understood
why the hired help, looking back
where he'd turned new hay
after their scythes,
had snickered into their sleeves;

he foresaw the hat-slapping,
doubled-up laughter of wags who traded
in wooden nutmegs,

and years later,
unbundling pure linen

he'd swapped for goods at the counter
of one country store or another,
discovering rocks at the center,

or here in the museum,
leaning on the case
where a monkey's head
stitched to a fishtail
was called the Feejee Mermaid,

he remembered Ivy Island,
the blacksnake rushing, its head
fixed at boy-height
sending him back over that fallen tree—

though this last
may have been a later embellishment,
the underlining
of one or another
of memory's transactions.

"Today You Will Meet the Love of Your Life"

If you think you already have,
revise your plans. Because
here it is in print
in your horoscope, inevitable
as Births and Obituaries,
a lot more serious than
Mary Worth. The stars
have set this one up, friend.
Hide from her under your car,
let's say, in your locked
garage, the least likely place,
and soon you'll be staring
at ankles that sent a dervish
down the straight and narrow.

Yes, it will happen today
and to you, though
you doubted the wisdom
of Rodgers and Hammerstein;
somebody has to get hit
with a meteorite some time.

But how are you going to go?
Casual? Formal? For two hours
you try combinations from
the closet, with front,
rear, and side views
that make you wish
you did situps.

Relax. It's inexorable.
By lunch each pretty face

will no longer be just that,
or the phone will unveil
a voice that touches
your spirit's lavender
more deeply than the final
seconds of dusk.

By midnight, nothing.
Gripping the bouquet
you sit up late, screen door
unlatched, house lit,
playing music that says
Don't even bother to knock.

In your dumb best suit
and tie, you feel like Anthony Quinn
in an old movie
of mandolins and vengeance.

Mrs. McCandless

Not knitting or peeling an onion,
but just sitting alone in her window,
like a grandmother doll in a box,
she saw the backyard through its changes,
how after Pearl Harbor the bocci court
erupted with salads and vines, how Keds
scuffling for basketballs trampled it
back flat, then each bedspring's arrival
among wedges of cement, after we left
for the curb in Gladehill Square.

Earlier, she'd seen me carried next door,
from the room over her head
where I was born. Same as the furniture
from floors above and below her:
something departed before something arrived.
Did she measure the months this way,
and the days by various laundries
squeaked out the lines and hauled
like survivors back through windows?

She watched Dixie Munzelle off to school daily
without a wave, as if foreknowing
I'd meet her again, not as the Statue of
Liberty on a chair in our sixth grade play,
but in strawberry blondes who danced
above my head, in a number of
topless versions of hell.

People just turned up in that triple decker.
Somebody's Uncle Ben could coax
halloween voices out of a carpenter's saw

with a table knife. When Milt Bevis
came home dressed as Government Property,
I begged to name the baby after him
till he knocked a drugstore over
and fled on foot. That same bad year
the kids of the bible-thumper
cheered while two dogs like piglets
parted a kitten from itself.

Through it all there was Mrs. McCandless,
her blue and white housedress
untroubled as the sky; though once,
in a dream, her eyes were the glass of lenses,
and she tossed my soul out her back door:
a gingerbread cookie stiff as bakelite
and buttoned with frosted X's.

Just in Case You're Wondering Who You Are

I am your little grandmother,
thief of the Queen's trout,
more oak and vinegar
than Mammy Yokum, but cold
as my white hair knot
for fear babies will grow
only as tall as typhus.

I keep the store in
the corner cellar, pick up
an acre here or there
like patchwork, and nurse
my forest people's paranoia.

My father's the one
whose skull's like
a scratched cobble
from trying to figure
how he dug a canal
and turned rocks into soil
with his Irish slide-rule.

After our trees fell down
and sailed away, our fields
fell down each year
and sailed away. With help
my father's house fell down
the day before the landlord
shook us off the estate
like crumbs from his shirtfront.
We followed the trees
and fields to Liverpool.

Reading the Obituaries

So Death is an unpromotable
cub reporter
at the desk in the corner
far away from windows,
who never gets
the human interest story.
He'll shave you clean,
deleting your lumpy
and colorful adjectives,
garbling the names
of your kids.
He'll box you in
to five Dick-and-Jane
paragraphs, erasing the words
you threw at somebody once,
and your motives, good
and bad. This rumpus
you barely ride herd on
is your life. Speak of it
kindly. Use your singular voice.

IV

Lying to Fall Warblers

Little questions of eyestripe,
wingbar and tail covert,
seed herds of the boreal fields
and aspen parks,

you who know heights
above water so green
no grass conveys it,

if I could learn
your slow, wheezy,
and ascending songs,
master their downward slurs
on the penultimate note,

I would tell you
how one year I intend
to plant bull and wavyleaf thistle
for you alone,
where now my squash leaves flop
like elephant ears.

So what if, overnight,
mushrooms have boiled up
through plush,
anthracite and Mr. Potatohead
breaking down woodpunk and leaf,

and a family of Indian pipes
wears peasant brown,

royalty turned out
of the summer palace?

When light slips south
along these natural threads
close to the ground,

let egrets nudge their young
from creek mouth to inlet
to warmer shallows.
What do they know?

Last night the Perseids
let stars go
in windfalls, and here you are,

ripe fruit filling the trees:
yellowthroat, blackpoll, bay breast,
flocks mixed as any
human motive,
names relearned for an hour.

Put by the urgency
we can't explain, and stay.
Teach *haute couture*
to the fish crow whose cry
is a New Year's horn
in his throat,

and manners to pinheaded jays.
Show chickadees
how to flare back at the sun.

Don't go skipping out
after that line of clouds

trotting east in light's
last tilt of rosé.

Night is a black wall,
and there are no Indies.
Stay here, under the steel edge
sweeping a way for rain.

A Few Words from the Weeds

When fields were pharmacies
you could brew an unguent here
to calm your swimming head,
or pulverize a stem
to salve your blotches.

Though you see us
as the dotage of lost dolls,
bearded, our sequins dulled,
or choruses of wallflowers,
loopy and dog-eared,
brained with autumn stars,

we have our ways:
driven from gardens
and the tracts of birds,
displaced with every
motion in the air,

we wait with brown
disguises in odd lots,
knowing the drift
of glass to be sand,

the rainy nibbling at
edges of asphalt, the unspoken
yielding of pharmacy to field.

The Last Open-Air Concert

One seems to have
a wheel and stick arrangement,
while others are forcing air
through tubes of grass.

But it's no cartoon
when tomatoes
show their seed teeth
and something has stained the leaves
on its mad
crash through to the West.

Those six-legged ones
must look like a living hieroglyph
in some alcove of the grass,
each urging
a tune out of itself:
rasp and pluck,
belly-thump,
vim of translucent wings.

Night and day they translate
inner solos, though now and then
one backs out,
leaving the shell of itself
to stand in,

or a leaf skids down,
cross-blocking a trio
into silence.

A raindrop
batting a trill, whole movements

dismantling in wind,
the ensemble thins
to some Spirit of '76
marching into a white barrage.

O last little stridulous frost-hung haiku,
when it's time, may each of us go as well.

Field

If only we could teach ourselves
to listen at its threshold,
what scores, what little wind-stars
out of papery goblets,
what squawks and piping
in its tuning up.
For the field too has its notes,
E F D G the weeds hold up.

"Don't be afraid
to be wrong," says the Famous
Conductor in the folder
you're probably opening
about now; and daughter, maybe
you think he'll fly out
and circle the room
where you're fitting your flute together
under the eye of Mr. Fearsome
Musicteacher.

Waiting outside where the field's
keys and clefs
cross and recross in a breeze
that sends scales drifting
above sow thistle and horsetail,
I'm sending you
the field's wide calm before you play.

Dog Love

Now the shadow of the wolf in him
wakes early. Before even a hairline of light
he paces the house, whining the sting
of each love dart till I wake
and begin weighing him with human analogies.
I know this wallowing in the soup of self,
that alphabet spelling me, me,
my insides flapping like a love-struck leaf,
all sense loping off on the heels
of every urge. When I unlock the dark
he goes straight for the woodpile
where the little bitch has set up
housekeeping. And he has unlocked
something I thought dead, the puritan
only sleeping in me: I could keep him
from kibble and scraps just to test
which hunger is stronger.

In the light rain before coffee
I whistle him back, but only part way,
relearning "hangdog" by the wet drape
of his ears. When he looks with concern
to the stacked wood, I hear the tearing
of our treaty, and meditate on guilt
and conditioning when he gives me a profile
but won't look me in the eye.
Will he seem older when she runs him off
snapping at his tendons, who has lured him
with love nips about the face?
She is not the one I would have chosen
for him, and at first, given her size,
I doubted the feasibility of it all.

But now I wonder if it's hot water
or cold you douse them with
before the schoolbus comes.

Owl-Struck

Like some red-faced god
rummaging in a barrel,
wind was tossing sparrows
over dune rims.
A morning for firesides
and splitting emotional hairs,
but I went out under geese
Canadian as the front,
their necks tensed
to rudders, and met
a herring gull on the flats
who picked up my pace,
sighting over his shoulder
as if my being there
made things serious.
He was smoky blue
instead of oyster-shell,
maybe changed by air
snapping its whips and flags.
I stopped speculating
on a white D.P.W. fencepost
miles from any highway
when the snowy owl
swiveled its glare on me,
and remembered northern
routes, and spirits
with harvest-moon eyes
swimming in and out of
headlight snow. Owl-struck,
they call it. My blood tree
shook in wind trying
to flail the browns

from dunegrass, and the owl
flew, as if I could tell it
something it didn't want to hear.

Mole

Before the first crisscross
of morning's business,
something shrugged
the concrete off and worked out
over ground it can't break
yet, nosing this contrail
across new snow, nursing its
pinhole vision with furred light.
Tacking away from walls
with an amoeba's
resolve, it dropped
to this step,
rose from this snow-angel
flutter—an embryonic pig
squinting at silence
before diving on.

The Brueghel Moment

On one of these afternoons,
in a lull between homecoming cars
I'll hear the yelping of hounds
and look up, before concentration
takes hold, to that hill across the way.
Through yellow-gray woodsmoke
flattening out of chimneys
there'll be figures
tending flames on that hill,
then hunters leaning homeward
in wind so cold it is
Time blowing to erase stone and glass.
A slide of flight across that scene,
a long-tailed bird planing
from trees, will be what shakes me.
Wobbling, a top-heavy skater
over slippery fear, I'll have entered
timelessness a moment,
inches from pratfall as always,
my residual peasantry
intact until commuter traffic resumes.

Pack Ice

Now I believe in Great Glooscap,
whose glacial arrowheads
these surely are, and any god
whose fists may have smashed
these ice tables to tablets.

Where the river
drains the harbor, there's
a sound like crumpling paper bags—
in a double harrowing
of the graveyards of ships
and sculpture, skiffs of ice
plow odalisques
and the busts of melting senators.

Milled to a conch
by the tongue-and-groovework
of water, a berg
has been stranded, its furrow
deep as a longship's keel rut.

Here at Icehenge
I will wait for the tide to turn,
line sundown up
with a megalithic doorway,
and wait for the first druid
crouching, moon-blue,
on the returning floe.

Listening by a Woodpile,
Night of Moon after Snow

Having done all I can for now
to these trees,
I almost hear the cold
drive a crackling star
through one face of a log
and out the other,

almost think I see
a shadow flick
into some hallway of oak
where the cat Blackie
sniffs, her tail flexing
the question of fieldmice.

I think of a snake's suit
hung on this bark
last September, and all of them
sleeping down there
in the dark, rolled tight as
the insides of baseballs.

In a few weeks I'll listen here
for killdeer off the river,
watch for their formal collars,
their rumps like moments of sundown
caught in iced cow prints
in the field across the way.

Then these mushroom-covered
chunks, that remind me

of oyster-bearing rocks,
will break to the fragrant
abiding scripture of the trees.

Winter Oysters

February: water and sky a gape
hinged at Great Island,
mudflats and cottages scoured
of summer, but a few car trunks
open to wire buckets and rakes
with serious teeth, and a few
aficionados of wind
sliding thick socks into waders
and hooking up, ready under hoods
and watch caps to break through
the tideline's rime, later
to break with short, upturned blades
into shells parted from rocks
and "dead man's fingers." This
is how we like them, not summer-thin
and weepy tourist fare, but hale
as innkeepers, their liquor clear,
fat with plankton that thrives
under a glaze drifting just below
green water, and without any
lemon sundrip or condiment
but a dash of bourbon to punctuate
each salty imperative.

Ellen's poem

Other Titles in the Contemporary Poetry Series